itty-bitty

IT'S ALL ABOUT JESUS!

WORD SEARCH PUZZLES

Warner Press Kids
educate • nurture • inspire

305800214195

Isaiah's Prophecy of a Child—the Messiah

Read the prophecy in Isaiah 9:6-7 (KJV) and find the words hidden in the puzzle.

CHILD	COUNSELLOR	INCREASE	ORDER
BORN	MIGHTY GOD	NO END	ESTABLISH
UNTO US	EVERLASTING	THRONE	JUDGMENT
GIVEN	FATHER	DAVID	JUSTICE
WONDERFUL	PRINCE OF PEACE	KINGDOM	FOREVER

O	G	M	K	M	O	D	G	N	I	K	Q	X	C	J
C	E	B	G	V	P	Q	O	R	D	E	R	Z	S	S
P	K	B	W	Q	Y	R	A	N	E	O	E	X	C	E
M	Q	S	U	O	T	N	U	X	L	K	V	W	A	C
B	X	Q	D	L	I	H	C	L	T	L	E	U	M	I
E	C	A	E	P	F	O	E	C	N	I	R	P	I	T
L	R	K	L	V	J	S	G	C	D	W	L	F	G	S
U	E	M	N	J	N	Z	S	I	C	E	A	F	H	U
F	V	T	R	U	D	N	V	Z	S	T	S	S	T	J
R	E	T	O	D	F	A	S	A	H	D	T	U	Y	T
E	R	C	B	G	D	A	E	E	N	U	I	S	G	H
D	O	S	Z	M	Q	R	R	E	T	X	N	F	O	R
N	F	T	Q	E	C	I	O	V	F	W	G	E	D	O
O	Y	S	Q	N	X	N	E	V	I	G	E	V	H	N
W	V	Q	I	T	H	S	I	L	B	A	T	S	E	E

(Answer on Page 42)

More Prophecies of Jesus Found in Old Testament

Read the prophecies about Jesus from Deuteronomy, Psalms, Jeremiah, Micah, and Zechariah. Find the words hidden in the puzzle.

PROPHET	BRANCH	LORD	REDEEMER	CHOSEN
WORDS	KING	SAVIOR	SERVANT	LIGHT
IN HIS MOUTH	REIGN WISELY	RULER	FATHER	GOD
COMMAND	JUDAH	ORIGINS	LAMB	BETHLEHEM
RIGHTEOUS	ISRAEL	ANCIENT TIMES	PRINCE	EPHRATHAH

Z	B	O	T	D	R	O	L	I	V	I	B	E	K	P
P	R	E	H	T	A	F	P	E	N	E	M	C	C	N
R	E	Z	G	K	E	P	C	H	T	S	S	G	O	E
O	M	K	R	F	A	N	I	H	O	E	W	P	M	S
P	E	Y	F	L	I	S	L	R	R	M	O	R	M	O
H	E	C	K	R	M	E	I	V	Z	I	R	E	A	H
E	D	U	P	O	H	G	A	G	G	T	D	I	N	C
T	E	B	U	E	I	N	D	N	N	T	S	G	D	Z
S	R	T	M	N	T	A	O	I	H	N	R	N	C	V
N	H	T	S	D	U	H	G	K	A	E	U	W	M	B
R	I	G	H	T	E	O	U	S	D	I	L	I	L	D
L	A	M	B	Y	B	K	T	X	U	C	E	S	I	G
P	U	N	R	O	I	V	A	S	J	N	R	E	G	Y
K	G	K	E	P	H	R	A	T	H	A	H	L	H	K
H	C	N	A	R	B	L	E	A	R	S	I	Y	T	Q

(Answer on Page 42)

The Parents of Jesus

Mary, Jesus' mother (Luke1), and Joseph, His father (Matthew 1:18-25), loved God very much. They obeyed God and became the parents of the Messiah.

BABY JESUS	MARRIED	VIRGIN	NAME HIM JESUS
MARY	DREAM	PREGNANT	PROPHECY
JOSEPH	ANGEL	EMMANUEL	NOT AFRAID
ENGAGED	SON	GOD WITH US	PROMISED
HOLY SPIRIT	GOD SAVES	OBEYED	GODLY

E	M	M	A	N	U	E	L	O	B	E	Y	E	D	T
N	P	A	T	D	N	G	F	F	B	J	N	D	M	N
W	C	D	Y	R	A	M	Q	D	A	O	N	R	M	A
L	O	E	P	D	R	L	Q	E	B	S	N	E	H	N
W	A	S	B	E	P	K	M	I	Y	E	I	A	O	G
G	Q	I	G	G	C	Y	D	R	J	P	G	M	L	E
J	R	M	O	A	S	I	F	R	E	H	R	D	Y	R
L	S	O	D	G	B	X	G	A	S	G	I	A	S	P
J	H	R	L	N	F	S	Z	M	U	O	V	N	P	P
P	U	P	Y	E	I	K	O	H	S	N	T	G	I	Q
E	E	V	G	O	D	S	A	V	E	S	F	E	R	S
N	A	M	E	H	I	M	J	E	S	U	S	L	I	F
V	L	B	N	O	T	A	F	R	A	I	D	F	T	S
K	T	N	G	N	S	U	H	T	I	W	D	O	G	S
W	F	Y	C	E	H	P	O	R	P	R	N	O	S	R

(Answer on Page 42)

Birth of Baby Jesus

Read about Jesus' birth in Luke 2:1-7, then find the words below in the puzzle.

BETHLEHEM	SHEPHERDS	PEACE	GALILEE
MARY	GREAT LIGHT	GOODWILL	NAZARETH
JOSEPH	GOOD NEWS	SHEEP	JUDAEA
STABLE	SAVIOR	DECREE	LINEAGE OF DAVID
HAY	CHRIST THE LORD	CAESAR AUGUSTUS	SWADDLING
MANGER	GLORY TO GOD	TAXED	CLOTHES

L	D	O	G	O	T	Y	R	O	L	G	V	X	U	R
E	D	K	C	B	H	T	E	R	A	Z	A	N	K	D
E	Z	D	L	D	M	E	H	E	L	H	T	E	B	X
L	D	R	O	L	E	H	T	T	S	I	R	H	C	Y
I	S	U	T	S	U	G	U	A	R	A	S	E	A	C
L	Y	H	H	Y	H	F	R	S	E	S	E	L	J	S
A	L	Y	E	N	R	E	W	L	E	A	L	B	O	W
G	N	I	S	U	G	A	P	T	R	V	B	H	S	E
P	N	U	W	N	D	E	M	H	C	I	A	A	E	N
E	I	N	A	D	R	E	C	I	E	O	T	Y	P	D
E	C	M	L	S	O	G	X	A	D	R	S	G	H	O
H	N	I	S	P	O	O	J	A	E	A	D	U	J	O
S	N	Z	S	Q	Z	A	G	H	T	P	D	S	N	G
G	G	E	E	G	R	E	A	T	L	I	G	H	T	V
L	I	N	E	A	G	E	O	F	D	A	V	I	D	F

(Answer on Page 42)

Simeon and Anna See the Messiah

Read the story in Luke 2:21-38 and find the words hidden in the puzzle.

EIGHT DAYS	LORD	BLESSED GOD	SERVED GOD
JESUS	SACRIFICE	HELD BABY	NIGHT AND DAY
ANGEL	TURTLEDOVES	DEPART	GAVE THANKS
PURIFICATION	YOUNG PIGEONS	ANNA	RETURNED
JERUSALEM	SIMEON	PROPHETESS	GALILEE
PRESENT HIM	HOLY GHOST	WIDOW	NAZARETH

```
Q H E L D B A B Y Q J P V Y Y
M Q E E L I L A G S E R S P A
R E T U R N E D K S G E E V D
S Y L A A N G E L E A S R P D
E E O A N S H R O T V E V U N
V H C U S N I D R E E N E R A
O D T I N U A M D H T T D I T
D D S E F G R M E P H H G F H
E E O V R I P E E O A I O I G
L P H R S A R I J R N M D C I
T A G H I E Z C G P K X J A N
R R Y K R R P A A E S Z E T Y
U T L W O D I W N S O V S I D
T D O G D E S S E L B N U O H
H D H P E I G H T D A Y S N U
```

(Answer on Page 42)

The Holy Family Makes Their Escape

Read about Mary and Joseph's escape in Matthew 2:13-18. Then find the listed words hidden in the puzzle.

ESCAPE	DREAM	OUT OF EGYPT	JEREMIAH
EGYPT	HEROD	CALLED MY SON	WEEPING
ANGEL	NIGHT	OUTWITTED	MOURNING
THE LORD	DEATH OF HEROD	MAGI	FLEE
JOSEPH	PROPHECY	BOYS	LAMENTATION
MARY	FULFILLED	BETHLEHEM	CHILDREN

N	W	E	E	P	I	N	G	D	L	E	G	N	A	N
N	O	I	T	A	T	N	E	M	A	L	O	R	K	M
A	M	Z	F	D	J	U	M	E	J	S	N	G	D	E
H	P	E	S	O	J	O	Q	H	Y	I	E	T	O	H
O	G	M	A	R	Y	C	W	M	U	O	R	P	R	E
Y	F	L	E	E	H	V	D	S	P	D	D	Y	E	L
F	H	U	W	H	T	E	Y	H	A	R	L	G	H	H
U	A	T	H	E	L	O	R	D	B	E	I	E	F	T
L	I	O	K	L	B	R	T	Y	G	A	H	E	O	E
F	M	K	A	N	I	G	H	T	M	M	C	C	H	B
I	E	C	T	P	Y	G	E	F	O	T	U	O	T	M
L	R	D	E	S	C	A	P	E	Q	L	L	Y	A	M
L	E	Y	U	M	O	U	R	N	I	N	G	G	E	K
E	J	E	P	R	O	P	H	E	C	Y	I	S	D	J
D	V	D	E	T	T	I	W	T	U	O	M	A	T	M

(Answer on Page 42)

Jesus as a Boy

When Jesus turned 12, He went with His parents and a large group to Jerusalem for Passover. On the way home, Jesus could not be found. Read the story in Luke 2:39-51.

JESUS	READ	TEMPLE	QUESTIONS
JOSEPH	WRITE	TEACHERS	OBEDIENT
WORKBENCH	STRONG	LISTENING	NAZARETH
WORSHIP GOD	WISDOM	ASKING	JERUSALEM
NAZARETH	PASSOVER	AMAZED	THREE DAYS
SCHOOL	TWELVE	UNDERSTANDING	GRACE
			FEAST

G	D	X	O	P	A	S	S	O	V	E	R	E	U	T
S	P	E	G	N	O	R	T	S	E	H	X	N	S	P
T	X	W	L	B	D	A	E	R	C	Q	D	A	T	S
S	N	D	O	P	Q	V	W	I	A	E	E	V	U	J
S	A	E	K	R	M	I	D	P	R	F	T	S	E	I
N	Z	K	I	U	S	E	A	S	G	E	E	R	U	S
O	A	G	A	D	Z	H	T	S	A	J	U	K	S	Y
I	R	T	O	A	E	A	I	C	K	S	H	C	J	A
T	E	M	M	A	N	B	H	P	A	I	H	N	O	D
S	T	A	S	D	W	E	O	L	G	O	N	C	S	E
E	H	O	I	R	R	O	E	R	O	O	T	G	E	E
U	C	N	I	S	M	M	Y	L	O	V	D	K	P	R
Q	G	T	G	N	I	N	E	T	S	I	L	D	H	H
Y	E	R	W	J	H	C	N	E	B	K	R	O	W	T
L	N	A	Z	A	R	E	T	H	E	V	L	E	W	T

(Answer on Page 43)

John Baptizes Jesus

John the Baptist was a strange guy, wearing clothes made from camel's hair and eating locusts and honey. UGH! But he was chosen by God for a special task. Read about it in Matthew 3:1-17.

REPENT	JORDAN RIVER	HOLY GHOST	VOICE
PREPARE	BAPTIZED	BURN	BELOVED
LORD	JESUS	CHAFF	SON
CAMELS HAIR	FIRE	FULFILL	WELL PLEASED
LOCUSTS	SANDALS	RIGHTEOUSNESS	DOVE
HONEY	WATER	HEAVENS OPENED	MIGHTIER

A	B	W	E	L	L	P	L	E	A	S	E	D	T	F
H	A	O	S	I	D	W	V	O	I	C	E	C	S	U
G	P	I	P	O	E	M	J	E	S	U	S	F	O	L
V	T	Y	R	W	N	W	I	D	R	J	F	F	H	F
S	I	U	E	A	E	W	X	G	O	A	Y	F	G	I
A	Z	P	P	T	P	O	S	R	H	E	X	D	Y	L
N	E	Z	A	E	O	F	D	C	N	T	R	U	L	L
D	D	M	R	R	S	A	A	O	L	O	I	P	O	P
A	S	V	E	S	N	N	H	C	L	I	V	E	H	O
L	Q	H	U	R	E	R	B	E	V	O	D	Q	R	W
S	V	J	I	E	V	U	K	V	R	E	P	E	N	T
L	I	V	R	Q	A	B	S	T	S	U	C	O	L	T
Z	E	I	E	E	E	D	E	V	O	L	E	B	X	K
R	F	R	I	G	H	T	E	O	U	S	N	E	S	S
X	H	K	R	I	A	H	S	L	E	M	A	C	V	Q

(Answer on Page 43)

Jesus' Disciples

The 12—different backgrounds, families and jobs. But all were called by Jesus to follow Him. They knew Jesus well— lived with Him, ate with Him, and they loved Him—but when He was arrested, they all disappeared. Read their stories in Matthew, Mark, Luke, and John.

SIMON	PHILIP	THADDAEUS	HEALED
PETER	BARTHOLOMEW	SIMON THE ZEALOT	CAST OUT DEMONS
JAMES	MATTHEW	JUDAS ISCARIOT	RAISED DEAD
JOHN	THOMAS	FISHERMEN	PREACHED
ANDREW	JAMES ALPHAEUS	TAX COLLECTORS	

C	A	S	T	O	U	T	D	E	M	O	N	S	C	S
I	Q	O	L	D	B	D	E	R	C	X	V	C	T	U
T	B	Y	T	Q	N	S	L	J	N	B	T	S	O	E
H	U	U	A	S	J	C	A	D	O	W	B	A	I	A
A	N	F	X	E	Q	O	E	H	M	D	A	M	R	H
D	G	Z	C	M	G	G	H	H	I	J	R	O	A	P
D	J	W	O	A	W	P	P	N	S	F	T	H	C	L
A	Y	O	L	J	P	H	I	L	I	P	H	T	S	A
E	T	O	L	A	E	Z	E	H	T	N	O	M	I	S
U	D	A	E	D	D	E	S	I	A	R	L	O	S	E
S	N	A	C	V	R	R	E	T	E	P	O	J	A	M
O	W	E	T	M	A	T	T	H	E	W	M	P	D	A
V	E	B	O	Z	W	E	R	D	N	A	E	S	U	J
V	D	P	R	E	A	C	H	E	D	D	W	G	J	B
H	Z	T	S	N	E	M	R	E	H	S	I	F	P	E

(Answer on Page 43)

The Ministry of Jesus

Jesus' ministry began when He was 30. He knew why God sent Him to earth. He taught, preached, healed, loved, and died for every one of us. See Luke 4.

TEACHING	DISCIPLES	SPIRIT	BREAD
MISSION	MIRACLES	WILDERNESS	WORSHIP THE LORD
HEALING	NAZARETH	TEMPTED	JERUSALEM
TOUCH	TRAVEL	FORTY DAYS	SON OF GOD
BAPTISM	CHILDREN	HUNGERED	ANGELS
GALILEE	PARABLES	STONES	DEPARTED

D	I	B	M	M	H	U	N	G	E	R	E	D	D	T
A	O	Q	W	T	I	L	G	S	K	D	T	R	I	I
E	M	G	X	T	E	R	E	A	E	T	O	R	W	R
R	H	U	F	V	M	L	A	T	L	L	G	I	W	I
B	Z	M	A	O	B	S	P	C	E	I	L	W	M	P
D	S	R	T	A	N	M	I	H	L	D	L	E	F	S
E	T	S	R	L	E	O	T	T	E	E	L	E	N	F
T	M	A	E	T	N	P	S	R	P	A	S	T	E	O
R	P	I	L	L	I	A	N	L	S	A	E	G	R	R
A	S	J	S	H	P	E	Z	U	E	A	B	N	D	T
P	Y	E	S	S	S	I	R	A	C	G	H	I	L	Y
E	M	R	N	S	I	E	C	H	R	C	N	L	I	D
D	O	P	V	O	J	O	I	S	U	E	E	A	H	A
W	P	J	J	F	T	N	N	O	I	V	T	E	C	Y
C	L	E	M	L	G	S	T	V	P	D	R	H	Z	S

(Answer on Page 43)

The Parables of Jesus

Jesus taught by telling parables/stories.
You can find 40 parables in the Gospels—Matthew, Mark, and Luke.

LAMP	OLD WINESKINS	PEARL	TALENTS
BOWL	SOWER	VINEYARD	MONEYLENDER
WISE	WEEDS	TWO SONS	GOOD SAMARITAN
FOOLISH	MUSTARD SEED	TENANTS	RICH FOOL
BUILDERS	HIDDEN TREASURE	WEDDING BANQUET	LOST COIN
NEW WINE	LOST SHEEP	FIG TREE	PRODIGAL SON

```
E R U S A E R T N E D D I H O
G R D E E S D R A T S U M L T
L O S T C O I N W E C Z D N U
P C O Z X S Y O H U X W W M Z
P N P D O F S F T Q I R I O R
R Y E W S O W E I N M I I N V
O S E W N A N X E A J C H E I
D R H S W A M S F B U H S Y N
I E S P N I K A T G F F I L E
G D T T L I N A R N I O L E Y
A L S P N W L E L I G O O N A
L I O S D E E W R D T L O D R
S U L M N L J C A D R A F E D
O B U T L W I S E E E N N R V
N J S L A M P M P W E L W O B
```

(Answer on Page 43)

The Good Samaritan

Read the story in Luke 10:30-37 and find the words from the story hidden in the puzzle.

MAN	STRIPPED CLOTHES	SAMARITAN	PAID FOR INN
JERUSALEM	LEFT HIM	TOOK PITY	DENARII
JERICHO	FOR DEAD	BANDAGED	REIMBURSE
ATTACKED	PRIEST	WOUNDS	EXPENSES
ROBBERS	PASSED BY	TOOK TO INN	NEIGHBOR
BEAT HIM	LEVITE	CARED FOR HIM	

S	E	S	N	E	P	X	E	R	I	T	I	E	D	N
A	T	T	A	C	K	E	D	D	Q	O	M	C	Z	N
M	M	R	S	Z	F	X	K	A	I	O	I	E	S	I
A	I	R	I	E	P	D	D	E	I	K	H	Q	D	R
R	H	E	O	P	I	Y	I	D	R	T	T	D	N	O
I	T	I	G	B	P	R	Q	R	A	O	A	J	U	F
T	F	M	V	J	H	E	P	O	N	I	E	E	O	D
A	E	B	S	Y	E	G	D	F	E	N	B	R	W	I
N	L	U	U	R	T	R	I	C	D	N	Q	I	P	A
J	V	R	A	S	E	I	U	E	L	H	L	C	A	P
U	S	S	L	Z	J	B	P	S	N	O	M	H	B	I
F	L	E	V	I	T	E	B	K	A	A	T	O	F	M
Y	B	D	E	S	S	A	P	O	O	L	F	H	B	A
R	D	E	G	A	D	N	A	B	R	O	E	M	E	N
C	A	R	E	D	F	O	R	H	I	M	T	M	C	S

(Answer on Page 43)

The Prodigal Son

Read the story in Luke 15:11-32 and find the hidden words from the story in the puzzle.

TWO SONS	FAMINE	SERVANTS	RING
YOUNGER	WHOLE COUNTRY	HAVE FOOD	CELEBRATE
WANTED HIS MONEY	NEEDY	GOING HOME	OLDER SON
TOOK OFF	HIRED	SINNED	ANGRY
WILD LIVING	FEED PIGS	FATHER RAN	LOST
SPENT ALL MONEY	HUNGRY	KISSED HIM	FOUND

N	E	Y	W	X	O	T	W	L	R	C	U	N	M	T
A	M	U	D	H	P	H	A	F	O	L	O	S	I	Y
R	O	W	O	E	O	A	N	L	C	S	E	N	H	G
R	H	O	I	A	E	L	T	C	R	L	T	O	D	F
E	G	O	H	L	S	N	E	E	Z	Q	Q	S	E	E
H	N	E	U	R	D	L	D	C	K	O	F	O	S	E
T	I	N	N	Y	E	L	H	L	O	M	O	W	S	D
A	O	I	G	B	O	A	I	G	G	U	U	T	I	P
F	G	M	R	D	V	T	S	V	R	I	N	G	K	I
W	G	A	Y	E	O	V	M	P	I	A	D	T	T	G
S	T	F	F	O	D	O	O	G	V	N	V	O	R	S
E	A	O	K	E	Q	C	N	R	A	N	G	R	Y	Y
J	O	O	R	Y	D	D	E	N	N	I	S	R	K	B
D	F	I	I	V	C	S	Y	Y	O	U	N	G	E	R
F	H	Y	E	N	O	M	L	L	A	T	N	E	P	S

(Answer on Page 44)

Jesus and the Beatitudes

Read the story in Matthew 5:3-12 and find the hidden words in the puzzle.

BLESSED	COMFORTED	FILLED	CHILDREN
POOR	MEEK	MERCIFUL	PERSECUTED
SPIRIT	INHERIT EARTH	MERCY	INSULT
KINGDOM	HUNGER	PURE HEART	SAY EVIL
HEAVEN	THIRST	SEE GOD	REJOICE
MOURN	RIGHTEOUSNESS	PEACEMAKERS	GREAT REWARD

```
Y L V N M O D G N I K H M R V
I P I P R H S J Y N D C E O T
R J E V D U U O G E R H R O Y
P I K A E O O N L V A I C P I
E K G D C Y G M G A W L Y D C
R C N H I E A E T E E D T E O
S T I N T N M S E H R R S L M
E R I O L E S A M S T E R L F
C A S R J U O U K E A N I I O
U E D N I E F U L E E G H F R
T H V M C P R I S T R K T O T
E E Z F G E S Y C N G S J I E
D R H T R A E T I R E H N I D
P U J B L E S S E D E S C X Y
X P R R H E A V E N T M S H U
```


(Answer on Page 44)

Salt and Light

Read Jesus' directions to us in Matthew 5:13-15. Find the words hidden in the puzzle.

SALT	GOOD	TOWN	BOWL
EARTH	THROWN OUT	BUILT ON HILL	PUT ON STAND
LOSES	TRAMPLED	CANNOT	EVERYONE
SALTINESS	UNDERFOOT	BE HIDDEN	LIGHT SHINE
SALTY AGAIN	LIGHT	LIGHT LAMP	SEE YOUR
NO LONGER	WORLD	PUT UNDER	GOOD WORKS
			GLORIFY FATHER

B	Z	E	N	O	Y	R	E	V	E	D	G	V	Q	R
U	T	O	W	N	R	E	G	N	O	L	O	N	E	V
I	F	W	T	R	A	M	P	L	E	D	S	H	S	D
L	P	M	A	L	T	H	G	I	L	E	T	G	S	T
T	T	O	N	N	A	C	S	I	E	A	O	A	E	O
O	T	Z	B	D	P	A	G	Y	F	O	L	Q	N	O
N	U	K	D	N	L	H	O	Y	D	T	O	Z	I	F
H	O	H	O	T	T	U	F	W	Y	B	I	T	T	R
I	N	T	O	B	R	I	O	A	S	E	S	O	L	E
L	W	R	G	O	R	R	G	A	C	S	M	A	A	D
L	O	A	A	O	K	A	Y	M	Z	S	K	F	S	N
W	R	E	L	S	I	N	E	D	D	I	H	E	B	U
O	H	G	F	N	E	N	I	H	S	T	H	G	I	L
B	T	G	G	P	U	T	O	N	S	T	A	N	D	L
W	O	R	L	D	W	P	U	T	U	N	D	E	R	V

(Answer on Page 44)

Wise and Foolish Builders

Read the story in Matthew 7:24-27 and in Luke 12:42-48.
Find the words hidden in the puzzle below.

EVERYONE	BUILT HOUSE	BEAT HOUSE	BEAT AGAINST
HEARS	ROCK	DID NOT FALL	HOUSE FELL
WORDS	RAIN CAME	FOUNDATION	GREAT CRASH
PRACTICE	STREAMS ROSE	FOOLISH MAN	
WISE MAN	WINDS BLEW	BUILT ON SAND	

R	G	E	B	D	L	T	E	K	B	L	E	W	E	N
O	H	B	E	E	I	L	F	M	U	W	N	O	M	G
C	H	E	A	K	S	D	E	C	A	F	I	W	A	R
K	F	B	T	S	D	U	N	F	U	C	A	O	C	E
P	O	E	H	T	N	N	O	O	E	H	R	R	N	A
R	O	A	O	R	A	G	A	H	T	S	N	D	I	T
A	L	T	U	E	S	E	S	M	T	F	U	S	A	C
C	I	A	S	A	N	E	V	R	E	L	A	O	R	R
T	S	G	E	M	O	O	Z	E	A	S	I	L	H	A
I	H	A	H	S	T	O	W	U	R	E	I	U	L	S
C	M	I	D	R	L	T	Z	I	V	Y	H	W	B	H
E	A	N	N	O	I	T	A	D	N	U	O	F	E	R
T	N	S	T	S	U	W	I	N	D	S	X	N	O	R
D	J	T	V	E	B	S	M	A	E	R	T	S	E	I
X	K	F	F	W	I	N	D	S	B	L	E	W	R	P

(Answer on Page 44)

The Rich Man and Lazarus

Read the story in Luke 16:19-31 and find the words hidden in the puzzle.

JESUS
DISCIPLES
LUXURY
BEGGAR AT GATE
LAZARUS
EAT SCRAPS
BEGGAR DIED
ANGELS TOOK HIM
ABRAHAM
RICH MAN DIED
TORMENT IN HADES
HAVE PITY
COOL TONGUE
WATER
AGONY IN FIRE
COMFORTED
GREAT CHASM
WARN FAMILY
MOSES
REPENT
WILL NOT LISTEN

W	A	T	E	R	G	R	E	A	T	C	H	A	S	M
S	T	O	R	M	E	N	T	I	N	H	A	D	E	S
S	U	S	E	J	C	R	S	H	E	J	N	J	F	W
Z	E	D	A	D	O	I	U	A	N	U	G	J	I	U
F	T	E	G	A	M	C	R	V	M	T	E	L	O	E
E	A	I	O	B	F	H	A	E	S	P	L	J	W	A
U	G	D	N	R	O	M	Z	P	V	N	S	R	A	T
G	T	R	Y	A	R	A	A	I	O	M	T	E	R	S
N	A	A	I	H	T	N	L	T	R	A	O	P	N	C
O	R	G	N	A	E	D	L	Y	V	H	O	E	F	R
T	A	G	F	M	D	I	H	J	T	A	K	N	A	A
L	G	E	I	S	S	E	S	O	M	R	H	T	M	P
O	G	B	R	T	X	D	G	P	X	B	I	N	I	S
O	E	U	E	L	U	X	U	R	Y	A	M	P	L	B
C	B	N	D	I	S	C	I	P	L	E	S	J	Y	H

(Answer on Page 44)

Servants Given Ten Minas

Read the story and find the words from Luke 19:11-27 hidden in the puzzle.

PARABLE	TEN MINAS	FIVE CITIES	TAKE OUT
JESUS	GOOD USE	TEN CITIES	REAP
JERUSALEM	GAINED	LAID AWAY	JUDGE
MAN	TEN MORE	CLOTH	OWN WORDS
NOBLE BIRTH	WELL DONE	AFRAID	DEPOSIT
SERVANTS	CHARGE	HARD MAN	INTEREST

```
D E P O S I T C L O T H S Q C
O T E N M I N A S Z Z E D P Y
W D N Z J N U V S M I C G A V
N E O G C B P O N T H T W X P
W N D S C A O A I A K A G R H
O I L G E U M C R V D K O B D
R A L R S D N G S I S E O M I
D G E I R E E K A J U O D Z A
S U W A T O S L E J S U U E R
E C H L T E N M O R E T S L F
F I V E C I T I E S J B E B A
J N A M S T N A V R E S G A Y
H T R I B E L B O N H O D R W
E H E X I N T E R E S T U A U
M E L A S U R E J M E R J P Y
```


(Answer on Page 44)

Miracles of Jesus

The 35 miracles Jesus performed are found in the four Gospels. Find the words taken from these stories hidden in the puzzle.

LEPROSY	SHRIVELED HAND	CRIPPLED	FOUR THOUSAND
SERVANT	BLIND MUTE	DROPSY	COIN IN FISH
MOTHER-IN-LAW	DAUGHTER	MAN AT POOL	FIG TREE
PARALYZED	BOY WITH DEMON	STORM	WATER TO WINE
BLEEDING	BLIND MEN	WALKED ON WATER	WIDOWS SON
POSSESSED	DEAF MUTE	FIVE THOUSAND	

R	E	T	A	W	N	O	D	E	K	L	A	W	V	N
H	O	D	M	O	T	H	E	R	I	N	L	A	W	O
F	M	E	T	U	M	D	N	I	L	B	D	L	P	M
H	A	L	N	B	L	E	E	D	I	N	G	O	Z	E
S	N	P	E	I	D	N	A	L	A	N	S	D	P	D
I	A	P	E	P	W	L	T	S	S	S	F	A	W	H
F	T	I	F	T	R	O	U	N	E	Q	R	U	I	T
N	P	R	I	L	U	O	T	S	A	A	I	G	D	I
I	O	C	G	S	H	M	S	R	L	V	W	H	O	W
N	O	N	T	T	M	E	F	Y	E	G	R	T	W	Y
I	L	D	R	O	D	C	Z	A	S	T	R	E	S	O
O	Z	U	E	R	O	E	E	T	E	P	A	R	S	B
C	O	N	E	M	D	N	I	L	B	D	O	W	O	C
F	I	V	E	T	H	O	U	S	A	N	D	R	N	B
S	H	R	I	V	E	L	E	D	H	A	N	D	D	Z

(Answer on Page 45)

Jesus Feeds 5,000

Read the story in Mark 6:35-44 and find the words hidden in the puzzle.

DISCIPLES	FIVE LOAVES	FIFTIES	SATISFIED
REMOTE	TWO FISH	HEAVEN	TWELVE BASKETS
LATE	DIRECTED	GAVE THANKS	LEFT
JESUS	PEOPLE SIT	BROKE BREAD	FIVE
FEED PEOPLE	GROUPS	DISTRIBUTE	THOUSAND
COST TOO MUCH	HUNDREDS	DIVIDED FISH	

```
S T I S E L P O E P S R G F S
E W E T U B I R T S I D H I K
L E D N A S U O H T B V C V N
P L T G S D E R D N U H U E A
I V M O C C W J A N R D M F H
C E N E M S A G E A E I O E T
S B R O K E B R E A D V O E E
I A D S T V R O N D B I T D V
D S C Q L A V U E S T D T P A
E K A E B O Y P V M W E S E G
T E F R D L K S A A O D O O W
A T D I R E C T E D F F C P H
L S S R V V E A H E I I P L A
S E I T F I F P N X S S N E M
S A T I S F I E D L H H B J P
```


(Answer on Page 45)

Jesus Walks on Water

Read the story in Matthew 14:22-33 and find the words hidden in the puzzle.

JESUS	ALONE TO PRAY	WALKED ON LAKE	REACHED HAND
SENT DISCIPLES	NIGHT	TERRIFIED	LITTLE FAITH
IN BOAT	BUFFETED	GHOST	WORSHIPED HIM
AHEAD	WINDS	COURAGE	SON OF GOD
DISMISSED	WAVES	BEGAN TO SINK	PETER
CROWD	DAWN	SAVE ME	WALKED ON WATER

W	A	L	K	E	D	O	N	W	A	T	E	R	Z	B
A	O	H	L	U	D	I	S	M	I	S	S	E	D	E
L	L	R	E	A	C	H	E	D	H	A	N	D	J	G
K	E	O	S	A	P	S	N	V	E	D	B	E	W	A
E	R	H	N	H	D	E	V	J	O	U	S	I	Y	N
D	E	T	F	E	I	L	Z	G	F	U	U	F	W	T
O	T	I	W	W	T	P	F	F	S	D	N	I	W	O
N	E	A	A	M	H	O	E	E	Z	A	U	R	V	S
L	P	F	V	A	N	T	P	D	G	I	V	R	H	I
A	T	E	E	O	E	W	R	R	H	A	T	E	J	N
K	H	L	S	D	W	O	R	C	A	I	R	T	M	K
E	G	T	Z	G	H	O	S	T	A	Y	M	U	Z	E
Q	I	T	T	T	A	O	B	N	I	L	G	G	O	X
G	N	I	V	C	J	M	N	W	A	D	W	A	G	C
S	E	L	P	I	C	S	I	D	T	N	E	S	X	U

(Answer on Page 45)

First Miraculous Catch of Fish

Read the story in Luke 5:4-11 and find the words hidden in the puzzle.

JESUS	CAUGHT NOTHING	HELP	ASTONISHED
SIMON	CAUGHT	FILLED BOTH	CATCH OF FISH
DEEP WATER	LARGE NUMBER	SO FULL	FISH FOR PEOPLE
LET DOWN NETS	NETS BREAKING	BEGAN TO SINK	LEFT EVERYTHING
MASTER	SIGNALED	FELL TO KNEES	FOLLOWED
ALL NIGHT	PARTNERS	SINFUL MAN	HIM

G	T	L	A	S	T	O	N	I	S	H	E	D	Q	H
M	N	F	N	L	S	N	A	M	L	U	F	N	I	S
B	Z	I	L	E	T	D	O	W	N	N	E	T	S	I
F	B	S	H	F	T	T	H	G	I	N	L	L	A	F
I	E	H	S	T	F	S	L	L	U	F	O	S	F	F
L	G	F	R	E	O	G	B	N	O	M	I	S	E	O
L	A	O	E	V	L	N	S	R	C	T	I	Z	L	H
E	N	R	N	E	L	O	T	C	E	G	X	M	L	C
D	T	P	T	R	O	S	T	H	N	A	A	V	T	T
B	O	E	R	Y	W	P	U	A	G	S	K	P	O	A
O	S	O	A	T	E	W	L	S	T	U	M	I	K	C
T	I	P	P	H	D	E	I	E	E	I	A	Q	N	H
H	N	L	U	I	D	V	R	J	H	J	D	C	E	G
O	K	E	H	N	Y	R	E	T	A	W	P	E	E	D
Z	L	A	R	G	E	N	U	M	B	E	R	A	S	A

(Answer on Page 45)

Jesus Calms a Storm

Read the story in Mark 4:35-41 and find the words hidden in the puzzle.

EVENING	FURIOUS SQUALL	SLEEPING	BE STILL
JESUS	WAVES	WOKE HIM	CALM
DISCIPLES	BROKE OVER BOAT	TEACHER	AFRAID
GO TO OTHER SIDE	NEARLY	CARE	NO FAITH
CROWD	SWAMPED	DROWN	TERRIFIED
BOAT	STERN	REBUKED WIND	

```
T B E W L D H D E G C S M C K
D Z L D Z T E E Y Z T E I A O
R S O L I N C P A K A L H L Q
O D U A A S W A M N O P E M T
W A F S L U R A R A B I K E E
N O X C E L Q E V E W C O V R
N G Z N K J I S H E W S W E R
D W O R C B Y T S T S I Y N I
R Y N E A R L Y S U O D L I F
E Z L T M X W U T E O O I N I
H D I S C I P L E S B I T G E
C V W E G N I P E E L S R O D
A U D A Z A F R A I D F O U G
E S E R E B U K E D W I N D F
T S B R O K E O V E R B O A T
```

(Answer on Page 45)

Jesus Casts Demons in Pigs

Read the story in Luke 8:26-39 and find the words hidden in the puzzle.

GERASENES	FELL	ABYSS	STEEP BANK
GALILEE	SHOUTING	HERD OF PIGS	DROWNED
JESUS	TORTURE	FEEDING	RIGHT MIND
DEMON	CHAINED	HILLSIDE	AFRAID
POSSESSED	UNDER GUARD	DEMONS BEGGED	CURED
CRIED	LEGION	HERD RUSHED	REGION

R	D	D	K	K	V	R	E	G	I	O	N	D	F	N
X	E	G	E	H	I	L	L	S	I	D	E	E	W	H
D	N	N	U	R	V	I	J	W	R	W	I	G	X	S
N	I	I	C	A	U	D	I	A	R	F	A	G	T	U
I	A	D	R	E	G	C	U	M	E	R	L	E	D	H
M	H	E	I	E	U	G	S	G	Z	E	E	B	S	E
T	C	E	E	M	R	H	A	Z	G	P	S	S	D	R
H	J	F	D	E	O	L	N	I	B	U	Y	N	R	D
G	J	L	D	U	I	O	O	A	S	B	B	O	O	O
I	K	N	T	L	M	N	N	E	A	Z	U	M	W	F
R	U	I	E	E	Q	K	J	X	M	H	M	E	N	P
W	N	E	D	E	S	S	E	S	S	O	P	D	E	I
G	E	H	H	E	R	D	R	U	S	H	E	D	D	G
E	U	H	E	R	U	T	R	O	T	F	E	L	L	S
S	A	I	G	E	R	A	S	E	N	E	S	E	N	W

(Answer on Page 45)

Jesus Heals an Official's Son

Read the story in John 4:43-54 and find the words hidden in the puzzle.

JESUS
GALILEE
PROPHET
FESTIVAL
CANA
ROYAL OFFICIAL
SON LAY SICK
CAPERNAUM
BEGGED JESUS
HEAL HIS SON
CLOSE TO DEATH
SIGNS
WONDERS
SON WILL LIVE
DEPARTED
SERVANTS
BOY WAS LIVING
YESTERDAY
FEVER LEFT
EXACT TIME
HOUSEHOLD
BELIEVED
SECOND
SIGN

D	D	S	U	S	E	J	D	E	G	G	E	B	L	R
R	N	H	T	A	E	D	O	T	E	S	O	L	C	D
F	O	O	Q	S	D	E	V	E	I	L	E	B	A	C
E	S	Y	C	H	O	U	S	E	H	O	L	D	P	F
S	S	H	A	E	J	N	G	C	A	N	A	C	E	E
T	I	P	S	L	S	D	W	A	R	O	G	R	R	V
I	H	G	R	E	O	S	E	I	L	C	B	C	N	E
V	L	S	N	O	R	F	U	T	L	I	Q	A	A	R
A	A	I	Z	E	P	V	F	S	R	L	L	V	U	L
L	E	G	D	B	Z	H	A	I	E	A	L	E	M	E
V	H	N	Y	W	P	V	E	N	C	J	P	I	E	F
I	O	S	T	E	X	A	C	T	T	I	M	E	V	T
W	K	C	I	S	Y	A	L	N	O	S	A	W	D	E
Y	E	S	T	E	R	D	A	Y	K	G	P	L	Y	A
B	O	Y	W	A	S	L	I	V	I	N	G	L	Z	N

(Answer on Page 46)

Jesus Heals a Paralytic

Read the story in Mark 2:1-12 and find the words hidden in the puzzle.

JESUS	NO ROOM LEFT	IN ROOF	TAKE MAT
FORGIVES	PREACHED	DIGGING	WALK
HEALS	PARALYZED	LOWERED MAT	SON OF MAN
CAPERNAUM	MAN	SINS FORGIVEN	AUTHORITY
PEOPLE	CARRIED BY FOUR	BLASPHEMING	FORGIVE
LARGE NUMBERS	OPENING	GOD	PRAISED GOD

T	F	E	L	M	O	O	R	O	N	E	V	A	A	D
C	A	R	R	I	E	D	B	Y	F	O	U	R	O	B
S	I	N	S	F	O	R	G	I	V	E	N	G	L	T
G	P	W	A	L	K	J	F	V	G	C	D	L	G	A
N	R	U	S	A	N	O	I	N	M	E	P	A	F	M
I	E	Z	B	B	R	N	I	C	S	E	A	R	O	D
G	A	V	Z	G	R	N	A	I	O	H	R	G	R	E
G	C	Q	I	O	E	P	A	P	E	E	A	E	G	R
I	H	V	O	P	E	R	L	A	P	G	L	N	I	E
D	E	F	O	R	P	E	L	C	Q	Z	Y	U	V	W
S	D	C	N	D	O	S	U	S	E	J	Z	M	E	O
B	L	A	S	P	H	E	M	I	N	G	E	B	S	L
T	U	Y	T	I	R	O	H	T	U	A	D	E	Z	E
M	K	J	T	A	K	E	M	A	T	R	G	R	X	B
G	O	D	M	A	N	A	M	F	O	N	O	S	N	U

(Answer on Page 46)

Jesus Heals a Woman in the Crowd

Read the story in Mark 5:25-31 and find the words hidden in the puzzle.

GERASENES	TWELVE	GREW WORSE	IMMEDIATELY
BOAT	YEARS	HEARD OF JESUS	STOPPED
LARGE CROWD	BLEEDING	TOUCHED HIS CLOAK	FAITH HEALED
FOLLOWED JESUS	SUFFERED	JUST TOUCH	GO IN PEACE
PRESSED	MANY DOCTORS	WILL BE	FREED
WOMAN	SPENT ALL	HEALED	

S	E	C	D	E	L	A	E	H	H	T	I	A	F	M
T	O	U	C	H	E	D	H	I	S	C	L	O	A	K
G	D	Y	H	E	A	R	D	O	F	J	E	S	U	S
E	L	D	E	B	L	L	I	W	P	E	U	Z	A	D
R	L	W	E	A	Y	X	Y	R	D	S	D	I	B	W
A	A	O	V	P	R	Q	E	T	E	R	E	G	L	J
S	T	R	D	X	P	S	M	J	R	O	E	N	E	U
E	N	C	U	E	S	O	D	T	E	W	R	I	E	S
N	E	E	A	E	L	E	T	Y	F	W	F	D	D	T
E	P	G	D	Z	W	A	W	S	F	E	L	E	I	T
S	S	R	B	O	A	T	E	S	U	R	E	E	N	O
R	V	A	L	I	L	P	R	H	S	G	J	L	G	U
C	Y	L	E	T	A	I	D	E	M	M	I	B	R	C
W	O	M	A	N	Y	D	O	C	T	O	R	S	M	H
F	T	W	E	L	V	E	C	A	E	P	N	I	O	G

(Answer on Page 46)

Jesus Heals a Man Born Blind

Read the story in John 9:1-12 and find the words hidden in the puzzle.

JESUS	WHO SINNED	NO ONE	WASHED
MAN	PARENTS	CAN WORK	POOL OF SILOAM
BLIND	WORKS OF GOD	LIGHT OF	CAME HOME SEEING
FROM BIRTH	DISPLAYED	THE WORLD	SIT AND BEG
DISCIPLES	DAY	SPIT	EYES OPENED
RABBI	NIGHT COMING	MUD	I COULD SEE

W	H	O	S	I	N	N	E	D	F	D	D	N	N	F
D	N	I	L	B	I	K	I	I	R	L	U	I	D	H
T	B	G	P	L	R	S	S	S	O	R	M	G	O	I
Z	X	F	X	O	P	J	B	C	M	O	S	H	G	C
U	L	M	W	L	I	E	D	I	B	W	T	T	F	O
G	Q	N	A	B	H	S	E	P	I	E	N	C	O	U
W	A	Y	B	M	B	U	N	L	R	H	E	O	S	L
C	E	A	A	N	J	S	E	E	T	T	R	M	K	D
D	R	N	U	D	J	H	P	S	H	F	A	I	R	S
M	A	O	L	I	S	F	O	L	O	O	P	N	O	E
M	N	O	O	N	E	Q	S	L	A	T	K	G	W	E
U	G	N	I	E	E	S	E	M	O	H	E	M	A	C
W	A	S	H	E	D	L	Y	A	D	G	Y	X	A	V
B	K	O	D	T	K	H	E	N	X	I	X	T	Z	A
R	G	E	B	D	N	A	T	I	S	L	S	P	I	T

(Answer on Page 46)

Jesus Cleanses Ten Lepers

Read the story in Luke 17:11-19 and find the words hidden in the puzzle.

JESUS
HEALS
TEN MEN
LEPROSY
JERUSALEM
STOOD
AT DISTANCE
LOUD VOICE
MASTER
PITY ON US
GO
SHOW YOURSELVES
TO PRIEST
CLEANSED
ONE
CAME BACK
PRAISING GOD
LOUD VOICE
THANKED
SAMARITAN
WHERE OTHER NINE
FOREIGNER
RISE
FAITH MADE
YOU WELL

F	S	E	V	L	E	S	R	U	O	Y	W	O	H	S
G	A	S	U	S	E	J	E	R	U	S	A	L	E	M
S	E	N	I	N	R	E	H	T	O	E	R	E	H	W
A	C	E	P	L	Y	E	V	T	N	E	M	N	E	T
M	L	C	R	F	O	O	D	Q	H	H	E	R	G	C
A	E	N	A	O	U	U	V	A	E	A	E	O	C	D
R	A	A	I	R	W	G	D	A	M	T	N	E	A	P
I	N	T	S	E	E	P	L	V	S	H	C	K	M	G
T	S	S	I	I	L	S	I	A	O	I	T	D	E	Q
A	E	I	N	G	L	E	M	T	O	I	O	I	B	D
N	D	D	G	N	C	S	P	V	Y	O	C	Z	A	K
N	E	T	G	E	C	B	D	R	T	O	J	E	C	F
J	S	A	O	R	C	U	F	S	O	O	N	E	K	Z
L	I	F	D	T	O	P	R	I	E	S	T	U	W	H
W	R	S	Z	L	O	G	D	G	T	E	Y	R	S	M

(Answer on Page 46)

Jesus Raises Lazarus from the Dead

Read the story in John 11:1-45 and find the words hidden in the puzzle.

LAZARUS	LORD	RABBI	FALLEN ASLEEP
SICK	WIPED FEET	STONE YOU	WAKE HIM UP
BETHANY	WITH HAIR	TWELVE HOURS	JESUS WEPT
MARY	SISTERS SENT WORD	DAYLIGHT	COME OUT
MARTHA	ONE LOVED IS SICK	NIGHT	CAME OUT ALIVE
POURED PERFUME	JUDEA	STUMBLE	

S	J	E	S	U	S	W	E	P	T	H	S	W	A	M
R	I	A	H	H	T	I	W	Y	I	R	W	E	K	K
C	M	S	Z	V	Y	E	N	Q	U	B	M	R	C	P
A	A	E	T	R	W	A	L	O	A	U	B	I	I	E
M	R	M	A	E	H	I	H	B	F	E	S	A	S	E
W	T	M	E	T	R	E	P	R	M	S	D	L	R	L
D	H	M	E	O	V	S	E	E	I	U	A	U	P	S
K	A	B	S	L	U	P	S	D	D	Z	T	U	J	A
T	K	Y	E	T	D	T	E	E	A	F	M	S	L	N
H	U	W	L	E	O	V	A	R	N	I	E	A	P	E
G	T	O	R	I	O	N	U	L	H	T	Z	E	L	L
I	S	U	E	L	G	S	E	E	I	A	W	O	T	L
N	O	U	E	M	V	H	K	Y	R	V	R	O	C	A
P	Z	N	I	G	O	A	T	U	O	D	E	A	R	F
M	O	T	Q	Y	W	C	S	Q	T	U	V	E	H	D

(Answer on Page 46)

Jesus Teaches How to Pray

Read the story in Matthew 6:5-14 and find the words hidden in the puzzle.

PRAY	PRAY TO FATHER	WILL BE DONE	KINGDOM
SYNAGOGUES	DONE IN SECRET	DAILY BREAD	POWER
STREET	REWARD YOU	FORGIVE US	GLORY
REWARD IN FULL	OUR FATHER	WE FORGIVE	
GO IN ROOM	HALLOWED NAME	TEMPTATION	
CLOSE DOOR	KINGDOM COME	DELIVER FROM EVIL	

L	I	V	E	M	O	R	F	R	E	V	I	L	E	D
B	L	Y	C	G	O	K	W	N	N	E	S	T	A	A
S	M	U	L	L	J	D	O	J	V	K	K	E	J	E
U	U	O	F	H	O	D	G	I	G	I	D	M	N	R
O	R	E	T	N	E	S	G	N	N	I	O	P	N	B
Y	S	B	V	B	I	R	E	G	I	O	C	T	S	Y
D	G	T	L	I	O	D	D	D	R	K	R	A	Y	L
R	P	L	R	F	G	O	R	N	O	K	O	T	N	I
A	I	O	E	E	M	R	I	A	F	O	O	I	A	A
W	E	W	W	C	E	O	O	R	W	P	R	O	G	D
E	V	T	O	E	G	T	Z	F	K	E	X	N	O	W
R	S	M	O	U	R	F	A	T	H	E	R	N	G	G
T	E	M	A	N	D	E	W	O	L	L	A	H	U	P
P	R	A	Y	T	O	F	A	T	H	E	R	L	E	K
D	O	N	E	I	N	S	E	C	R	E	T	T	S	F

(Answer on Page 47)

Jesus Sees Zacchaeus

Read the story in Luke 19:1-10 and find the words hidden in the puzzle.

JESUS	CLIMBED	CAME DOWN	GIVE HALF
JERICHO	SYCAMORE TREE	WELCOMED JESUS	TO POOR
ZACCHAEUS	SEE JESUS	PEOPLE	PAY BACK
TAX COLLECTOR	COME DOWN	MUTTERED	FOUR TIMES
WEALTHY	STAY AT YOUR HOUSE	GUEST	SALVATION
SHORT	TODAY	SINNER	COME

Z	S	S	H	V	L	O	F	L	A	H	E	V	I	G
M	A	V	E	V	N	W	O	D	E	M	O	C	J	D
S	Y	C	A	M	O	R	E	T	R	E	E	R	K	M
I	H	Q	C	C	I	H	B	S	P	V	X	O	C	V
Z	T	H	U	H	G	T	C	G	H	J	E	O	A	R
P	L	Y	T	A	A	M	R	I	F	O	I	P	B	E
V	A	E	L	P	O	E	P	U	R	Z	R	O	Y	N
H	E	G	U	E	S	T	U	Z	O	E	R	T	A	N
N	W	O	D	E	M	A	C	S	A	F	J	P	P	I
A	S	U	S	E	J	E	E	S	T	O	D	A	Y	S
S	U	S	E	J	D	E	M	O	C	L	E	W	H	M
B	N	R	T	A	X	C	O	L	L	E	C	T	O	R
C	O	M	E	S	A	L	V	A	T	I	O	N	I	I
X	M	U	T	T	E	R	E	D	E	B	M	I	L	C
S	T	A	Y	A	T	Y	O	U	R	H	O	U	S	E

(Answer on Page 47)

Jesus and God Love Us

Read the story in 1 John 4:7-21 and find the words hidden in the puzzle.

ONE ANOTHER	ATONING	WE OUGHT	CONFIDENCE
BORN OF GOD	SACRIFICE	TO LOVE GOD	JUDGMENT
KNOWS GOD	FOR OUR SINS	GOD LIVES	NO FEAR
GOD SENT SON	FRIENDS	IN US	LOVE BROTHER
TO THE WORLD	GOD SO	GOD IS LOVE	LOVE SISTER
LIVE THROUGH HIM	LOVED US	COMPLETE	

M	K	N	O	W	S	G	O	D	N	W	E	K	L	T
E	I	E	T	E	L	P	M	O	C	H	C	D	O	O
V	S	H	S	F	H	S	S	S	K	S	N	O	V	T
O	E	Z	H	D	L	T	G	D	E	A	E	T	E	H
L	V	F	R	G	N	U	P	O	O	C	D	O	S	E
S	I	T	O	E	U	E	L	G	Q	R	I	L	I	W
I	L	J	S	R	H	O	I	Y	Q	I	F	O	S	O
D	D	D	U	S	O	T	R	R	R	F	N	V	T	R
O	O	W	D	D	S	U	O	H	F	I	O	E	E	L
G	G	H	P	O	G	U	R	N	T	C	C	G	R	D
N	O	F	E	A	R	M	D	S	A	E	M	O	P	R
W	E	O	U	G	H	T	E	E	I	E	V	D	M	I
G	N	I	N	O	T	A	X	N	V	N	N	I	J	N
D	O	G	F	O	N	R	O	B	T	O	S	O	L	U
L	O	V	E	B	R	O	T	H	E	R	L	I	A	S

(Answer on Page 47)

THE LAST SUPPER

Read the story in Matthew 26:17-25 and find the words hidden in the puzzle.

UNLEAVENED BREAD	BETRAY ME	SON OF MAN	FORGIVENESS
DISCIPLES	DIPPED HIS HAND	RABBI	OF SINS
PREPARATIONS	INTO BOWL WITH ME	BREAD	FATHERS
PASSOVER	JUDAS	MY BODY	KINGDOM
APPOINTED TIME	AS WRITTEN	CUP	MOUNT OF OLIVES
RECLINING		BLOOD OF COVENANT	HYMN

T	N	A	N	E	V	O	C	F	O	D	O	O	L	B
M	Y	B	O	D	Y	G	R	E	V	O	S	S	A	P
D	H	U	A	S	W	R	I	T	T	E	N	Y	P	A
S	C	U	P	S	R	E	H	T	A	F	G	B	M	H
N	J	O	G	N	I	N	I	L	C	E	R	U	Y	M
I	N	T	O	B	O	W	L	W	I	T	H	M	E	Y
S	U	E	M	Y	A	R	T	E	B	P	N	M	S	K
F	P	R	E	P	A	R	A	T	I	O	N	S	R	I
O	S	S	E	N	E	V	I	G	R	O	F	A	V	N
T	G	V	N	A	M	F	O	N	O	S	B	U	J	G
U	N	L	E	A	V	E	N	E	D	B	R	E	A	D
M	O	U	N	T	O	F	O	L	I	V	E	S	A	O
V	E	M	I	T	D	E	T	N	I	O	P	P	A	M
E	K	D	N	A	H	S	I	H	D	E	P	P	I	D
D	I	S	C	I	P	L	E	S	A	D	U	J	K	H

(Answer on Page 47)

The Crucifixion

Read the story in Matthew 27:15 - 30 and find the words hidden in the puzzle.

CONDEMNED	FIELD OF BLOOD	PILATE	WASHED HANDS
JUDAS	GOVERNOR	INNOCENT MAN	FLOGGED
RETURNED SILVER	CHOSEN BY CROWD	EXECUTED	SCARLET ROBE
CHIEF PRIESTS	BARABBAS	CRUCIFY HIM	CROWN OF THORNS
BURIAL PLACE	MESSIAH	WHAT CRIME	SPIT
			HIT HIM

R	E	V	L	I	S	D	E	N	R	U	T	E	R	F
M	C	D	E	N	M	E	D	N	O	C	T	K	K	I
S	A	B	B	A	R	A	B	E	W	A	P	D	R	E
T	L	M	S	A	D	U	J	M	L	R	W	V	Y	L
S	P	R	D	H	I	T	H	I	M	O	Z	H	D	D
E	L	O	N	G	T	J	P	R	R	B	Q	A	E	O
I	A	N	A	M	T	N	E	C	O	N	N	I	G	F
R	I	R	H	D	D	G	Y	T	S	B	U	S	G	B
P	R	E	D	Q	G	B	F	A	W	N	P	S	O	L
F	U	V	E	V	N	J	O	H	W	I	I	E	L	O
E	B	O	H	E	X	E	O	W	T	I	K	M	F	O
I	S	G	S	C	A	R	L	E	T	R	O	B	E	D
H	D	O	A	Q	M	I	H	Y	F	I	C	U	R	C
C	H	V	W	V	U	M	D	E	T	U	C	E	X	E
C	R	O	W	N	O	F	T	H	O	R	N	S	D	Y

(Answer on Page 47)

The Crucifixion, Part 2

Read the rest of the story in Matthew 27:31-54 and find the words hidden in the puzzle.

SOLDIERS	IN FEET	TORN TOP TO BOTTOM	TOMBS OPENED
MOCKED	KEPT WATCH	BODIES CAME	BODIES RAISED
SIMON	THIS IS JESUS	FROM TOMBS	CENTURION SAID
CARRIED CROSS	KING OF JEWS	EARTH SHOOK	SURELY HE WAS
GOLGOTHA	UP SPIRIT	ROCKS SPLIT	
NAILS IN HANDS	TEMPLE CURTAIN		

M	Q	S	S	U	R	E	L	Y	H	E	W	A	S	C
O	R	T	H	C	T	A	W	T	P	E	K	S	C	E
T	O	M	B	S	O	P	E	N	E	D	D	N	A	N
T	C	U	S	W	E	J	F	O	G	N	I	K	R	T
O	K	B	P	S	I	M	O	N	A	A	C	F	R	U
B	S	O	D	S	M	A	B	H	T	S	R	G	I	R
O	S	D	O	E	P	P	N	R	X	O	G	O	E	I
T	P	I	B	H	K	I	U	F	M	L	P	L	D	O
P	L	E	M	Q	S	C	R	T	M	D	T	G	C	N
O	I	S	H	L	E	H	O	I	S	I	E	O	R	S
T	T	C	I	L	Q	M	T	M	T	E	E	T	O	A
N	O	A	P	X	B	N	N	R	D	R	F	H	S	I
R	N	M	G	S	J	I	U	G	A	S	N	A	S	D
O	E	E	D	E	S	I	A	R	S	E	I	D	O	B
T	H	I	S	I	S	J	E	S	U	S	G	A	B	E

(Answer on Page 47)

He's Alive!

Read the Resurrection story in Luke 24:1-12 and find the words hidden in the puzzle.

FIRST DAY	NO BODY	HE HAS RISEN	STRIPS LINEN
OF WEEK	CLOTHES GLEAMED	TOLD APOSTLES	LAYING THERE
WOMEN	STOOD BESIDE THEM	DID NOT BELIEVE	WONDERING
TOOK SPICES	BOWED DOWN FACES	NONSENSE	WHAT
WENT TO TOMB	TO GROUND	PETER	HAPPENED
STONE ROLLED AWAY	NOT HERE	RAN TO TOMB	

S	T	O	O	D	B	E	S	I	D	E	T	H	E	M
T	E	B	M	O	T	O	T	N	A	R	W	V	N	W
O	A	C	L	A	Y	I	N	G	T	H	E	R	E	N
N	N	H	A	W	O	N	D	E	R	I	N	G	N	R
E	D	E	W	F	O	T	N	J	L	O	T	E	I	F
R	N	W	S	T	N	O	D	E	U	F	T	S	L	T
O	U	K	H	I	B	W	B	R	X	W	O	N	S	O
L	O	E	D	O	R	T	O	Y	R	E	T	E	P	O
L	R	O	D	M	O	S	J	D	D	E	O	S	I	K
E	G	Y	A	N	Z	F	A	L	D	K	M	N	R	S
D	O	W	D	X	C	R	H	H	P	E	B	O	T	P
A	T	I	H	A	P	P	E	N	E	D	W	N	S	I
W	D	E	M	A	E	L	G	S	E	H	T	O	L	C
A	T	O	L	D	A	P	O	S	T	L	E	S	B	E
Y	A	D	T	S	R	I	F	T	W	O	M	E	N	S

(Answer on Page 48)

Jesus Leaves Instructions

Read the story in Matthew 28:16-20 and in Acts 1:4-8.
Then find the words hidden in the puzzle.

GREAT	WORSHIPED	GO	SON
COMMISSION	HIM	MAKE	HOLY SPIRIT
ELEVEN	DOUBTED	DISCIPLES	TEACHING
DISCIPLES	AUTHORITY	NATIONS	OBEY
GALILEE	HEAVEN	BAPTIZING	COMMANDED
MOUNTAIN	EARTH	FATHER	WITH YOU

Y	A	E	E	L	I	L	A	G	Y	S	Y	P	U	C
D	Y	P	G	M	U	A	N	A	T	I	O	N	S	M
S	H	X	B	U	O	Y	H	T	I	W	H	R	B	J
M	E	O	K	P	B	D	E	F	R	Z	N	C	A	S
O	L	L	L	R	E	R	K	A	O	G	E	O	P	E
U	W	H	P	Y	Y	L	A	T	H	O	V	M	T	L
N	V	O	E	I	S	S	M	H	T	M	E	M	I	P
T	L	G	R	A	C	P	L	E	U	G	L	I	Z	I
A	I	N	M	S	V	S	I	R	A	F	E	S	I	C
I	I	I	I	C	H	E	I	R	Q	P	O	S	N	S
N	H	H	H	T	E	I	N	D	I	N	A	I	G	I
V	T	C	X	M	A	G	P	E	V	T	O	O	O	D
G	R	A	X	O	S	Y	T	E	D	S	C	N	B	X
J	A	E	D	E	T	B	U	O	D	G	R	E	A	T
T	E	T	S	H	D	E	D	N	A	M	M	O	C	E

(Answer on Page 48)

Jesus Ascends to Heaven

Read the story in Acts 1:9-12 and look for the words hidden in the puzzle.

JESUS	INTENTLY	WHY DO YOU STAND	JERUSALEM
TAKEN UP	SKY	LOOKING	MOUNT OF OLIVES
FROM SIGHT	SUDDENLY	COME BACK	SABBATH
CLOUD	TWO MEN	SAME WAY	DAYS WALK
HID HIM	DRESSED IN WHITE	HEAVEN	
LOOKING	STOOD BESIDE	APOSTLES	

H	Y	M	O	U	N	T	O	F	O	L	I	V	E	S
D	I	K	C	O	M	E	B	A	C	K	L	T	Q	Q
M	R	D	S	N	K	F	H	T	I	X	F	W	T	Y
E	S	E	H	O	H	L	W	E	M	U	H	Q	H	T
L	A	P	S	I	T	O	A	S	A	Y	S	E	G	B
A	B	C	Y	S	M	N	U	W	D	V	S	Z	I	I
S	B	L	S	E	E	D	I	O	S	E	E	B	S	N
U	A	O	N	A	D	D	Y	G	L	Y	W	N	M	T
R	T	U	K	E	M	O	I	T	N	N	A	V	O	E
E	H	D	N	J	U	E	S	N	A	I	V	D	R	N
J	Z	L	E	S	E	O	W	K	W	K	K	S	F	T
D	Y	S	T	J	P	O	W	A	Y	H	E	O	D	L
F	U	A	V	A	L	B	Z	Q	Y	L	I	N	O	Y
S	N	V	D	L	O	O	K	I	N	G	U	T	U	L
D	R	S	T	O	O	D	B	E	S	I	D	E	E	P

(Answer on Page 48)

Page 3

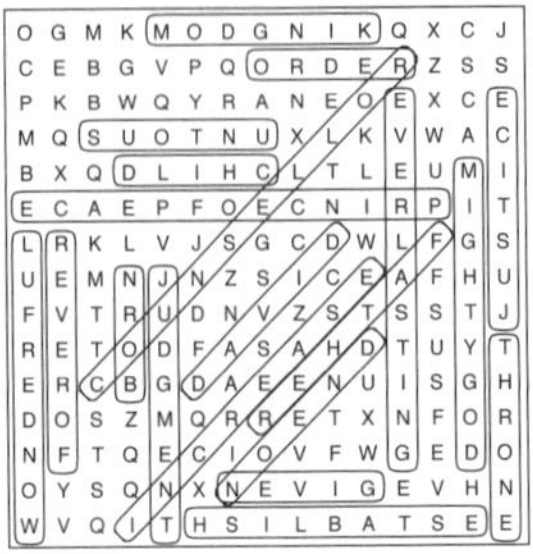

Page 4

Page 5

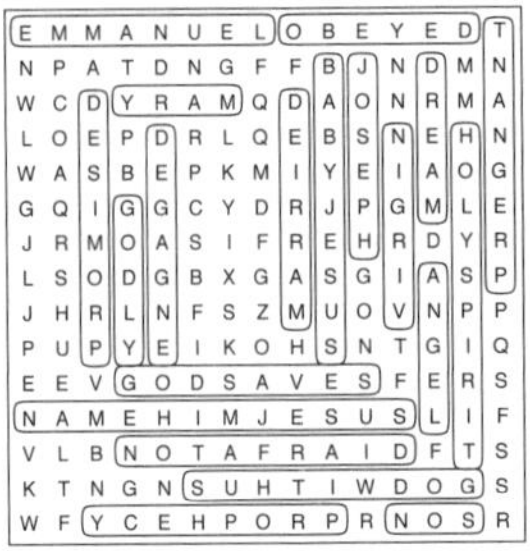

Page 6

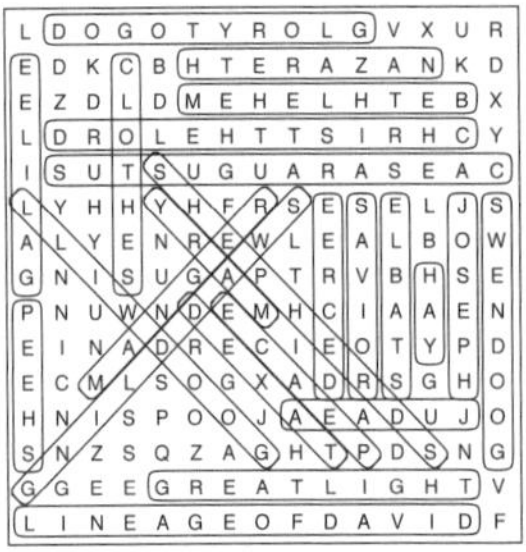

Page 7

Page 8

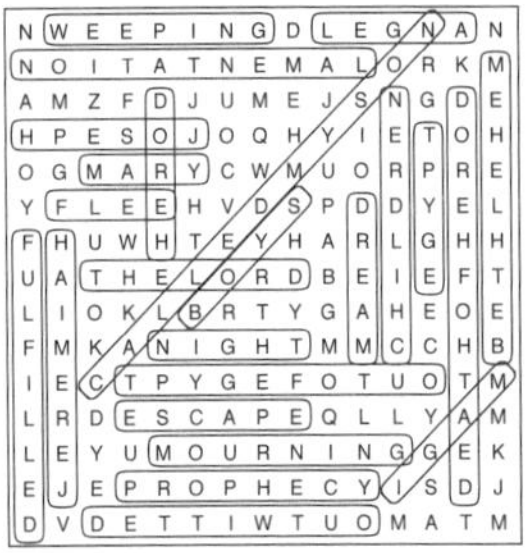

Page 9

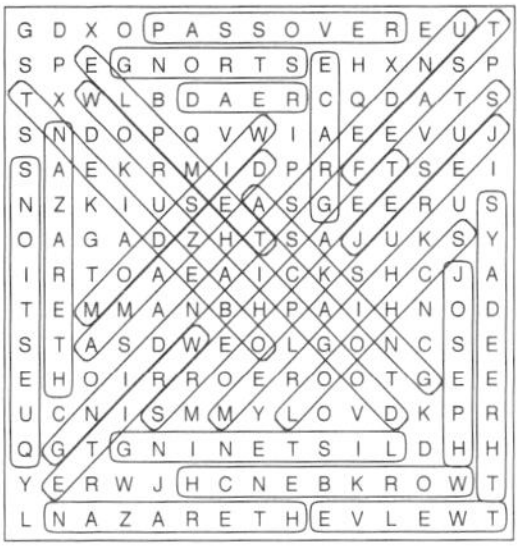

Page 10

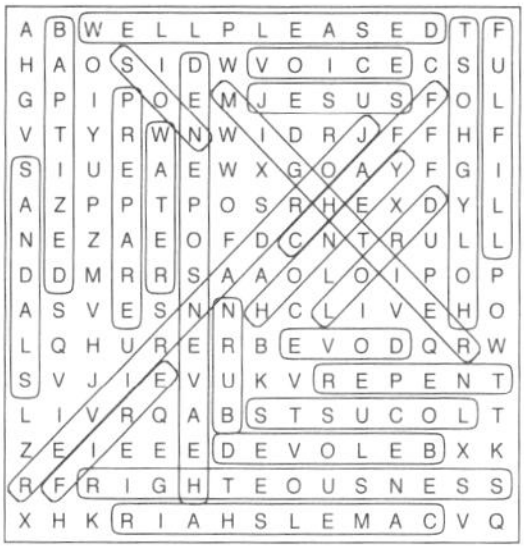

Page 11

Page 12

Page 13

Page 14

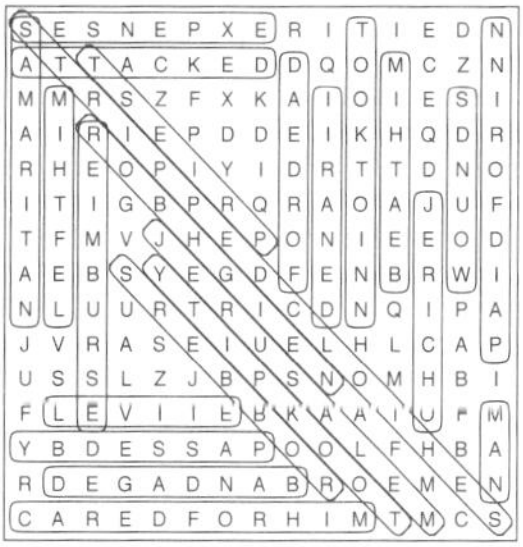

Page 15

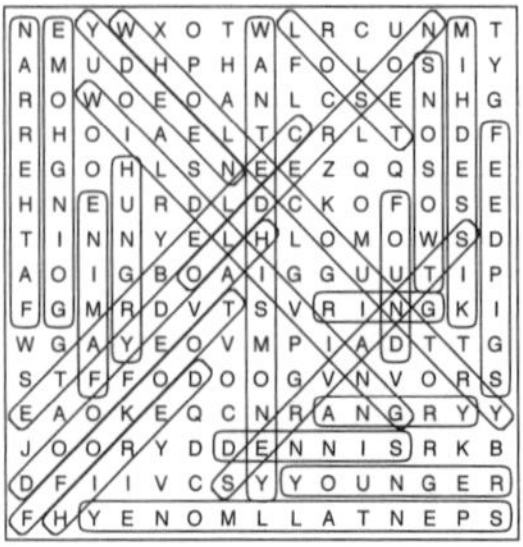

Page 16

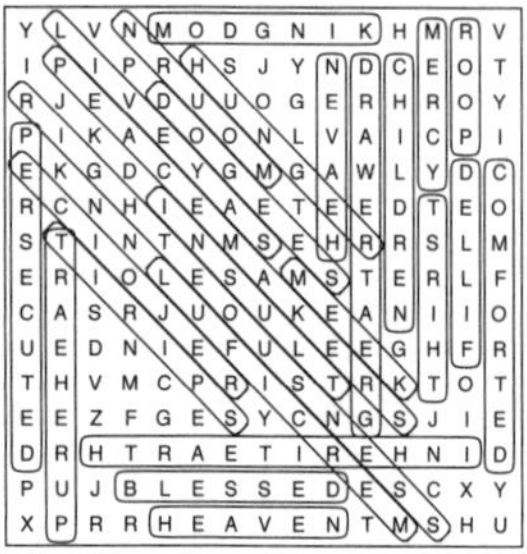

Page 17

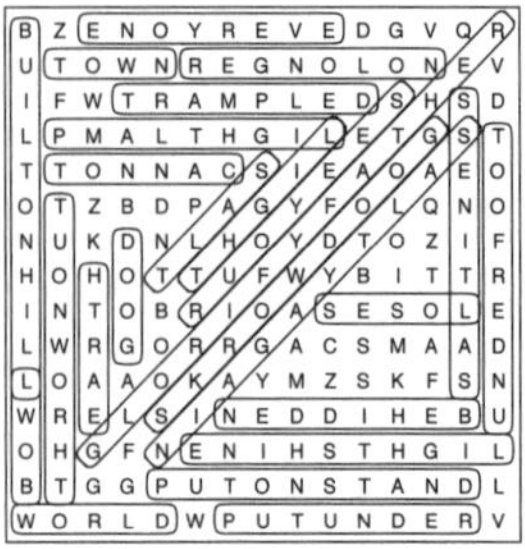

Page 18

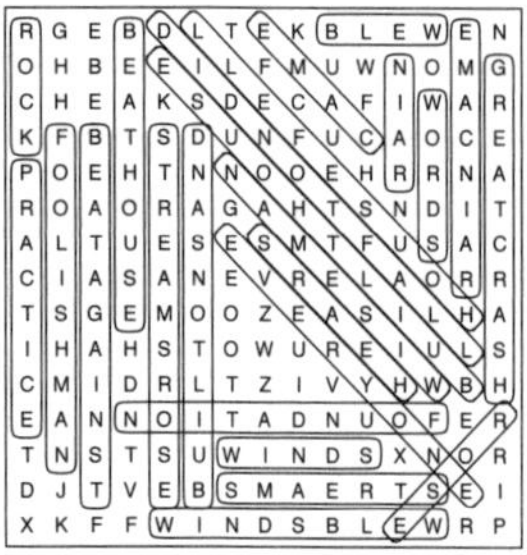

Page 19

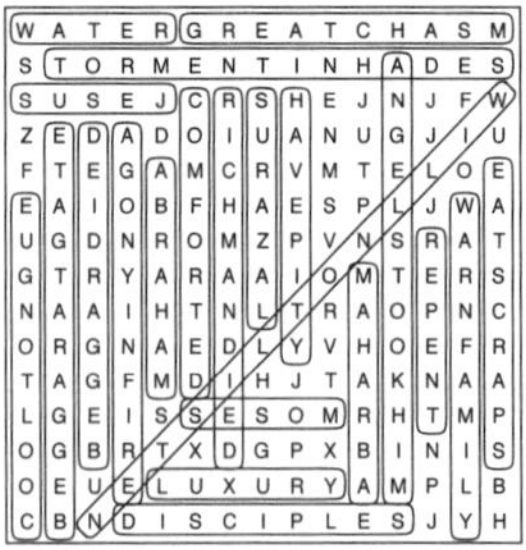

Page 20

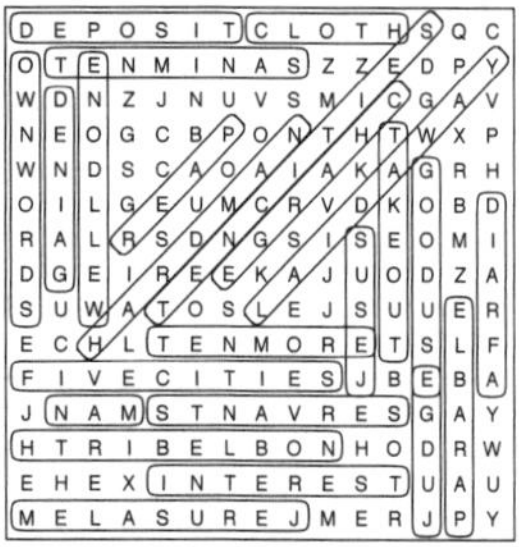

Page 21

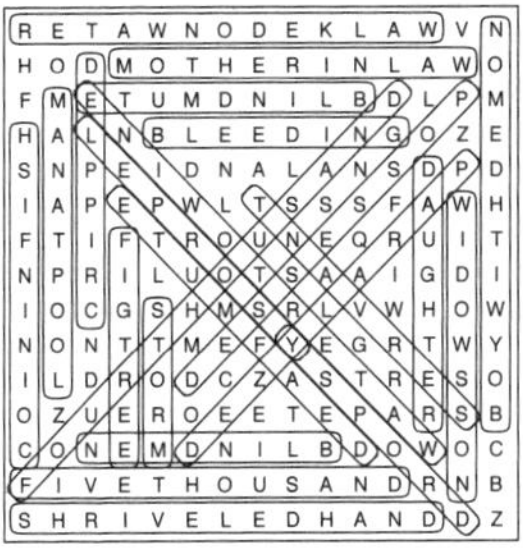

Page 22

Page 23

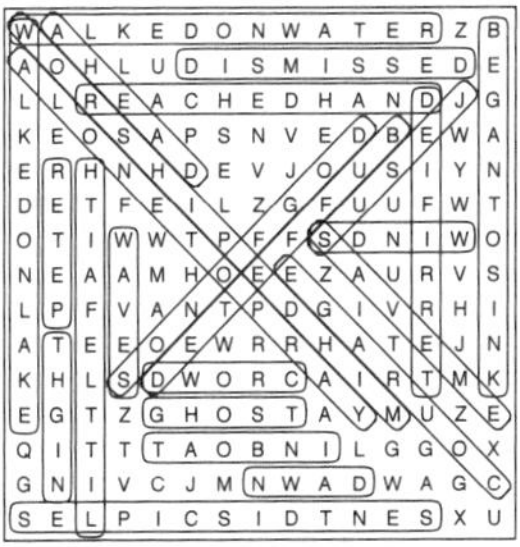

Page 24

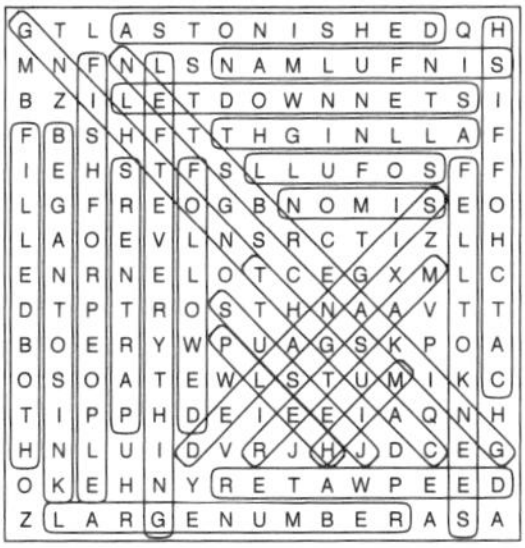

Page 25

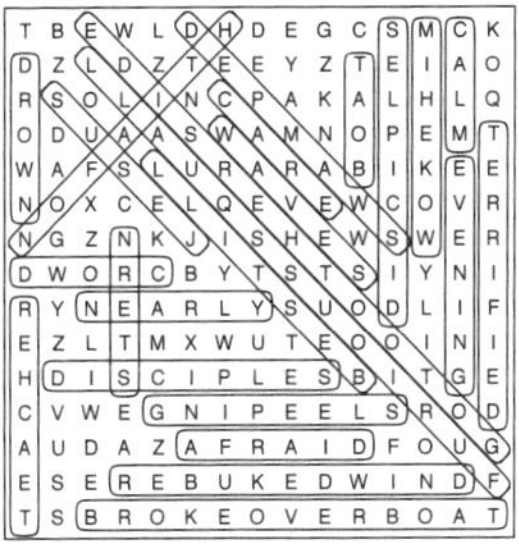

Page 26

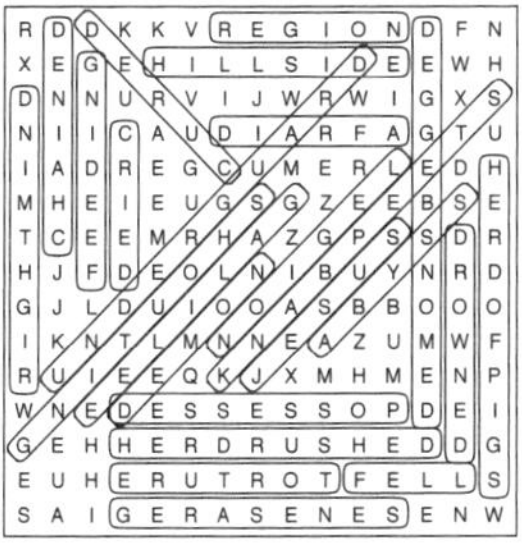

Page 27

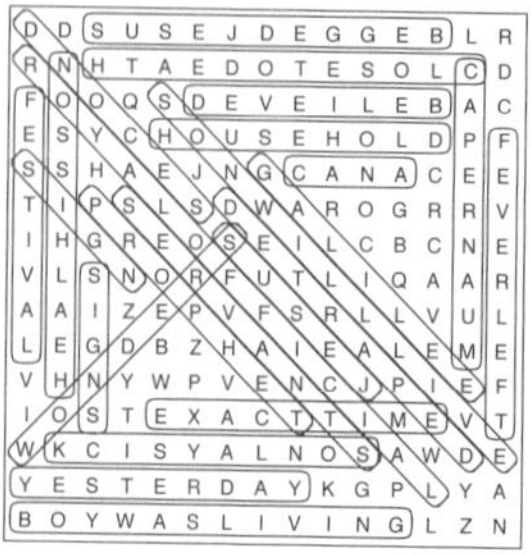

Page 28

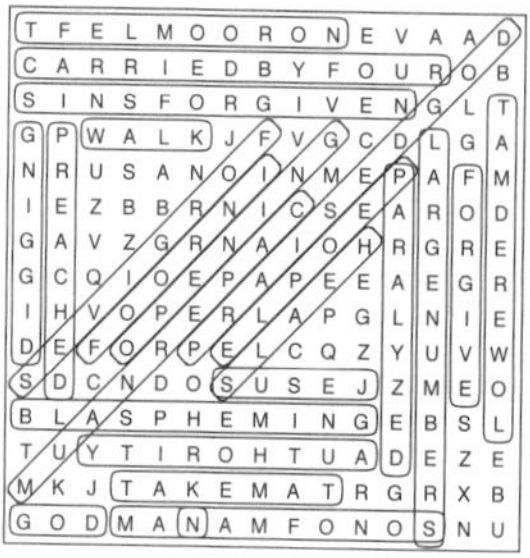

Page 29

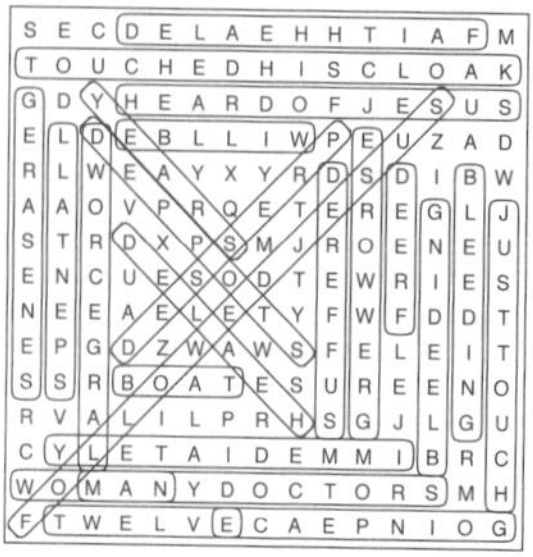

Page 30

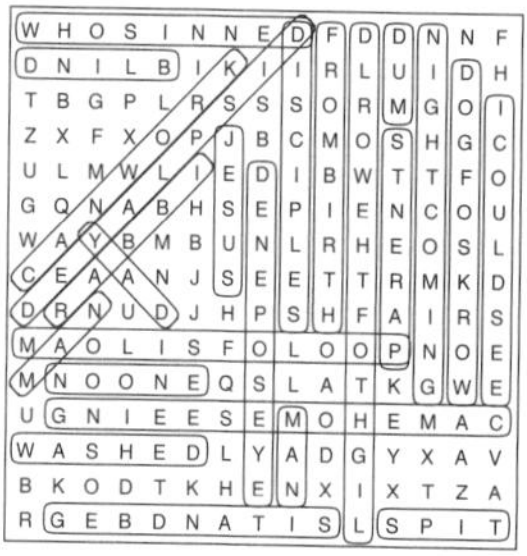

Page 31

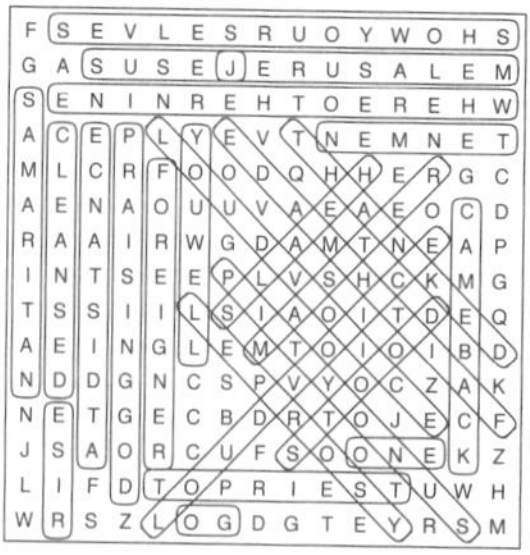

Page 32

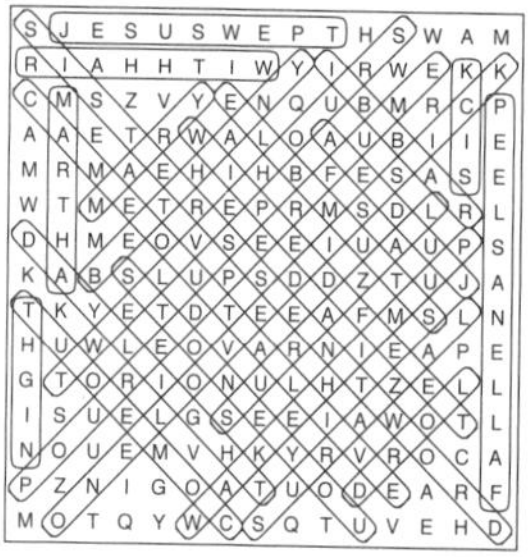

Page 33

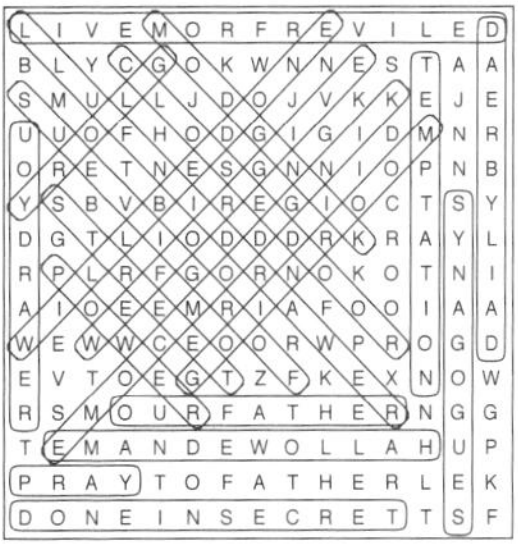

Page 34

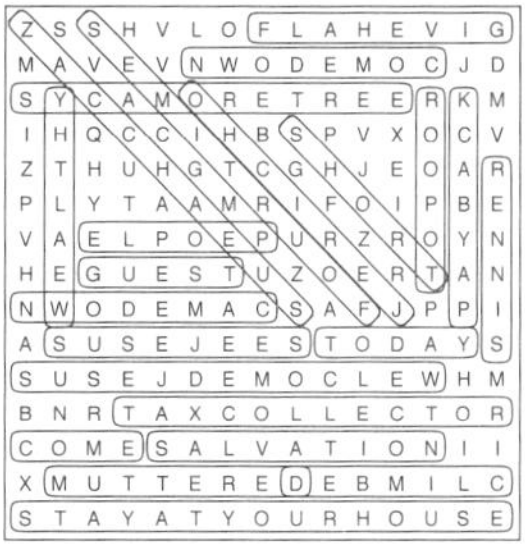

Page 35

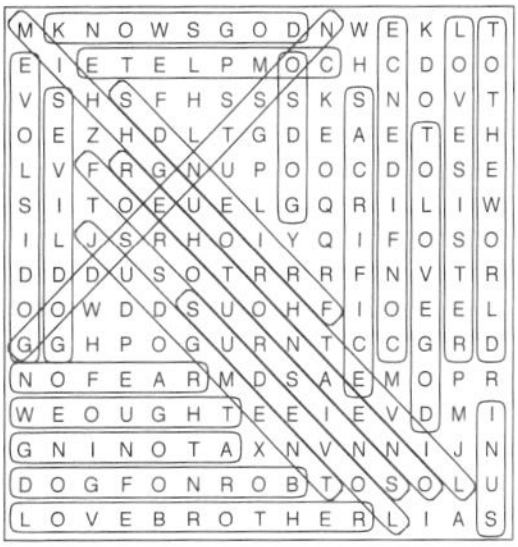

Page 36

Page 37

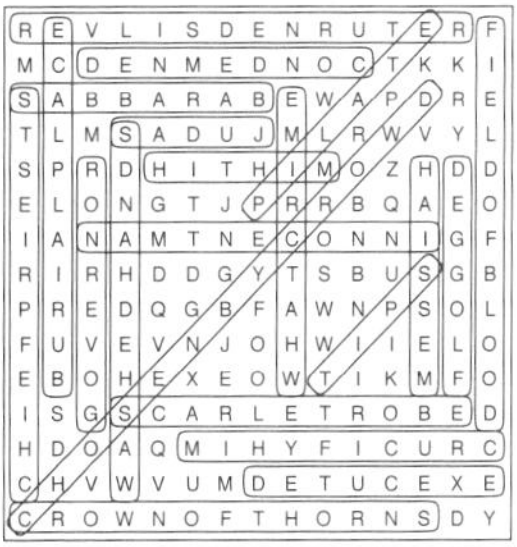

Page 38

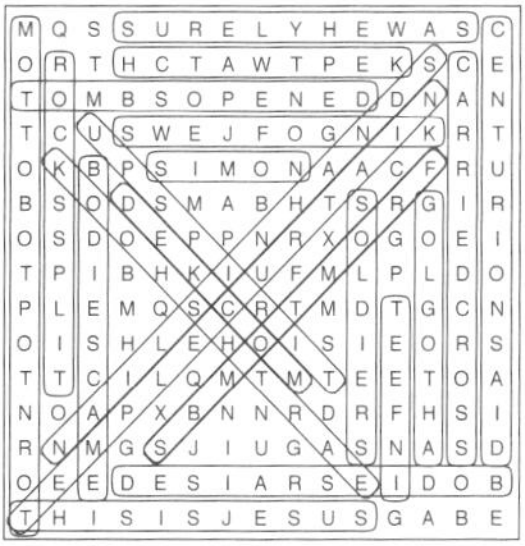

Page 39

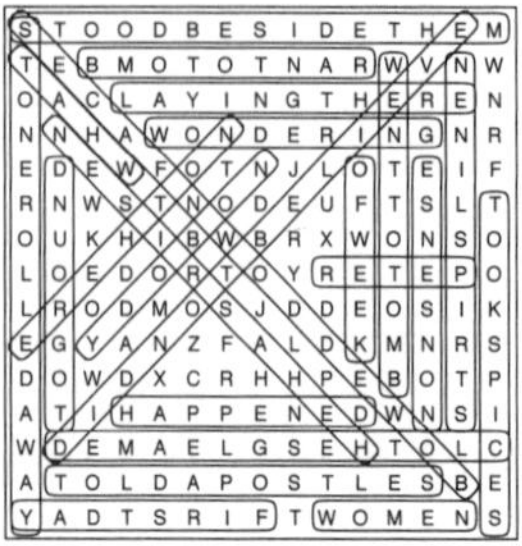

Page 40

Page 41

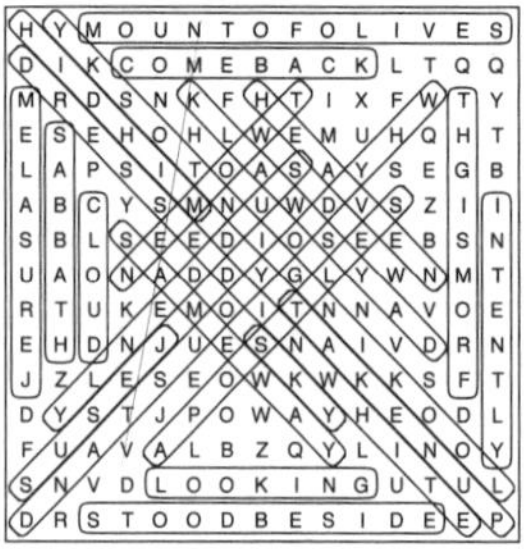